■ SCHOLASTIC
**News**
**Nonfiction Readers**

# Math on the Playground

## by Ellen Weiss

Children's Press®
A Division of Scholastic Inc.
New York  Toronto  London  Auckland  Sydney
Mexico City  New Delhi  Hong Kong
Danbury, Connecticut

These content vocabulary word builders are for grades 1–2.

Math Consultant: Linda K. Voges, EdD, Cohort Coordinator/Lecturer, College of Education, The University of Texas at Austin

Reading Consultant: Cecilia Minden-Cupp, PhD, Early Literacy Consultant and Author, Chapel Hill, North Carolina

Photographs © 2008: Alamy Images: 21 (Chris Gibson), 4 bottom left, 5 bottom right, 9 top (Nieh imagebroker), 5 top right, 7 (Zak Waters); Corbis Images/Andrea Rugg Photography/Beateworks: Ellen B. Senisi: back cover, 5 bottom left, 9 bottom; JupiterImages/Bananastock: 1, 11, 13; PhotoEd (Michelle D. Bridwell), 4 bottom left, 5 top left, 16 (Michael Newman); Superstock, Inc./Purestock: c Illustrations by Kathy Petelinsek

Book Design: Simonsays Design!
Book Production: The Design Lab

Library of Congress Cataloging-in-Publication Data
Weiss, Ellen, 1949–
Math on the playground / by Ellen Weiss.
p. cm.—(Scholastic news nonfiction reader)
Includes bibliographical references and index.
ISBN-13: 978-0-531-18533-9 (lib bdg.)  978-0-531-18786-9 (pbk.)
ISBN-10: 0-531-18533-8 (lib bdg.)  0-531-18786-1 (pbk.)
1. Mathematics—Juvenile literature. 2.Playground—Mathematics—
Juvenile literature. I. Title. II. Series.
QA40.5.W45 2008
510—dc22                    2007000972

# CONTENTS

# WORD HUNT

Look for these words as you read. They will be in **bold**.

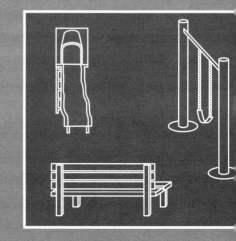

## diagram
(**dye**-uh-gram)

## rectangle
(**rek**-tang-guhl)

## ruler
(**roo**-lur)

**measure**
(**meh**-zhur)

**playground**
(**play**-ground)

**triangles**
(**tri**-ang-guhlz)

**shapes**
(shayps)

# Playing with Math

Let's play with math!

The **playground** is one of our favorite places.

There are lots of ways we can use math there.

How would you use math on this playground?

You can look for **shapes** on the playground.

The sandbox is a **rectangle**. It has four sides. Two sides are long. Two sides are short.

Look at the climbing dome. Can you see the **triangles**?

What other shapes can you see?

Turn to page 23 for the answer.

You can count at the playground, too.

Ella counts the number of times she jumps rope.

She wants to set a new record.

You can jump rope and do math at the same time!

Yesterday, Ella jumped 53 times.

Today, she jumped 6 times more than that.

How many times did she jump?

Turn to page 23 for the answer.

**53 + 6 = ?**

These two boys are going to play on the seesaw.

One of them weighs 38 pounds (17 kilograms).

The other weighs 46 pounds (21 kilograms).

Whose side is heavier?

Turn to page 23 for the answer

46 pounds

38 pounds

Is 46 pounds more or less than 38 pounds?

Let's find out how big our playground is.

First, we have to **measure** the playground.

Sometimes we measure using a **ruler**. Today we will measure using steps.

There are 8 steps from the bench to the slide.

**ruler**

slide

8 steps

bench

We measured three parts of the playground.

This **diagram** shows the parts we measured.

It is 14 steps from the slide to the swing.

How many steps is it from the swing to the bench?

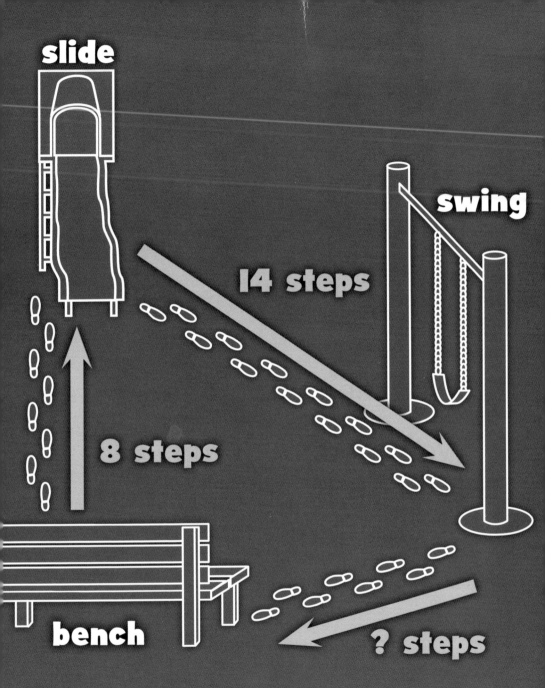

slide

swing

14 steps

8 steps

bench

? steps

19

Look at the sign.

What time does the playground close?

The playground is closing soon.

It is time to go home.

We had a lot of fun with math today at the playground!

Turn to page 23 for the answer.

**Try to find other ways to use math when you go to the playground.**

Playground Hours
•8:00 am – 6:00 pm•

# YOUR NEW WORDS

**diagram** (**dye**-uh-gram) a simple picture that shows the parts of something

**measure** (**meh**-zhur) to figure out how long, wide, or heavy an object is

**playground** (**play**-ground) an outdoor area where children can play

**rectangle** (**rek**-tang-guhl) a shape with four sides and four right angles

**ruler** (**roo**-lur) a long, flat piece of wood or plastic that is used for measuring things and drawing straight lines

**triangles** (**tri**-ang-guhlz) shapes with three sides and three angles

**shapes** (shayps) the forms or outlines of objects

# ANSWERS

## Page 8
Some other shapes in the picture are a circle, a star, and an oval.

## Page 12
Ella jumped 59 times.
**53 + 6 = 59**

## Page 14
The child who weighs **46** pounds is heavier.
**46** pounds is more than **38** pounds.

## Page 18
It is **8** steps from the swing to the bench.

## Page 20
The playground closes at **6 PM**.

# INDEX

## FIND OUT MORE

**Book:**

Stamper, Judith Bauer, and Chris Demarest (illustrator). *Go Fractions!* New York: Grosset & Dunlap, 2003.

**Website:**

Math Arcade
*www.funbrain.com/brain/MathBrain/MathBrain.html*

## MEET THE AUTHOR

Ellen Weiss has received many awards for her books for kids. She lived in England for a short time, where people say "maths" instead of "math."